Grace Kelly

True Stories of a Psychological Phenomenon

Dr. Julia Sanders

Table of Contents

Grace Kelly –The Anti-Cinderella

Introduction

Whenever one hears of a prince finding a bride without royal blood, inevitably, the term "Cinderella" pops up. On one side, a wealthy, handsome prince in search of love. On the other, a guileless, virginal, anonymous woman of lower station, "common" but with a wholly uncommon beauty and charm. She sweeps him off his feet. They fall in love. He moves heaven and earth to find her. They marry and live happily ever after.

In the case of Grace Kelly – Hollywood beauty turned Her Serene Highness, Princess Consort of Monaco after her well-publicized, well-packaged storybook marriage to Prince Rainier III – the Cinderella reference is easy to make, but far from accurate. All too many key points of the narrative just are not there.

For one thing, Prince Charming had a complex lineage that counted among his relations, the daughter of a laundress. He was also heir to a kingdom that was floundering in economic problems, and under threat from its powerful neighbors and competitors. Whether he had intended it or not – for some rumors do suggest Rainier might have been actively seeking a marketable American bride – the Prince's marriage to a superstar was one way of putting his little principality on the world map and setting his grand plans for its revival into motion. Thus, in this fairy tale? There may have been love, but there could have also been the less romantic notion of function.

Second, the "Cinderella" of our tale was neither anonymous nor needy – Grace Kelly was a successful Hollywood actress and an Academy Award winner, yes, but she had also come from a wealthy Philadelphia family. Ever heard of Cinderella paying a $2 million dowry to marry her Prince Charming? Well that is what the Kellys had to do when their daughter Grace married Rainier III. Reportedly, her family footed half of the money and she was successful enough to handle the rest herself.

As for guileless and virginal... Hollywood's reigning ice queen had a beautiful, stony countenance but she was a passionate conqueror underneath. She was rumored to be a heartbreaker, a man-eater who went through not only plenty a leading man, but she didn't even spare the married ones.

More importantly? When Rainier III married Grace Kelly, he did not quite elevate her to his station. They had something more of a partnership. He may have given her a title and a position, but she was instrumental in elevating the image of his country by her name and innate glamour. She was the one who made her new position modern, relevant and enviable. She made "Princess of Monaco" mean something fresh and extraordinary. Monaco, at the time, was somewhat in decline and has also been known as 'a sunny country for shady people.' But simply because *the* Grace Kelly was its Princess, there was something about the locale that was elegant and desirable. In so many ways, she became ambassadorial.

The "Cinderella" connection would be inaccurate for one more reason – happily ever after was all too temporary. Grace Kelly's life was cut short by a car accident in 1982. The Princess was only 53 at the time, much too young and still so beautiful. As of this writing, the country she had made her home still stands, also beautiful and still prosperous, but not immune from scandal. The beautiful royal family she left behind have all been caught in each of their own controversies.

Her son, Prince Albert II, fathered illegitimate children with different women when he was a bachelor. Just before his wedding in 2011, the family had to deny rumors that his wife-to-be, Charlene Whittstock, was caught at the airport trying to flee – it was just one of several alleged escape attempts she was trying to make to after realizing the extent of his indiscretions.

Prince Rainier and Princess Grace's daughters, Caroline and Stephanie, have complicated love lives of their own. Caroline has married thrice; one ending in divorce, another ending in a tragic death, and her current one at an estrangement with a troubled man. Stephanie, on the other hand, had marriages and divorces with her bodyguard and a trapeze artist. She also has several children conceived out of wedlock.

Ironically, Princess Grace's children mired in a series of romantic misfortunes might be one of the few, vaguely aspects of Grace

Kelly's story resembling a fairy tale – for if family lore holds true, a curse was once set upon the Grimaldis wherein they would never have real happiness in marriage. If this holds true, then Albert II< Carlone and Stephanie may just be the most recent casualties in a line long plagued by romantic scandal and tragedy. This curse would also be blamed for the Princess' untimely death, by people who may believe in such things. Whether or not one subscribes to this belief is immaterial. Perhaps there is a curse afoot, perhaps it is simply a way of attempting to understand the seemingly improbable number of romantic hardships borne by a single family. Either way, early death and a troubled family life are hardly anyone's idea of happily-ever-after.

In this and in many ways, Grace Kelly is the anti-Cinderella. She is made no less beautiful and no less glamorous by this, however. If anything, her depth and complexity, and how she and her family have tried to weather the storms in their lives, makes them even more interesting and worthy of knowing.

Early Life

Grace Patricia Kelly was born on the 12th of November, 1929, in Philadelphia, Pennsylvania. She was one of John Brendan "Jack" Kelly, and Margaret Katherine Majer's four children – one boy and three girls. Grace was the ill-fitting middle daughter.

Jack and Margaret were very athletic. He was a three-time gold medalist for the United States' Olympic rowing team, and is in the U.S. Olympic Hall of Fame. She was a champion collegiate swimmer, and in University of Pennsylvania, she was a physical education instructor and the Ivy League school's the first coach for the women's teams. The Kelly family was prosperous not for their feats in sports, however. Jack was a self-made millionaire, the son of an immigrant bricklayer and a former laborer himself, turned contractor who owned a lucrative brick business in the East Coast. He had even built the family's stately, 2 and 1/2 –story brick, Georgian mansion in Philadelphia. It had a playhouse and a tennis court, which in the winters were iced over for skating.

Jack had his eyes set not only on financial success but establishing himself and his family within their well-heeled community. He worked hard, but was also busy with sports and politics. One of his political achievements was to be elected into the City Council. He had grand dreams for his children, too, and he and his wife had an intense style of motivating them. The Kelly parents were hard to please and encouraged competition among the siblings – allegedly, competing even for the love of mom and dad. The Kellys required discipline and obedience, and though they employed household servants, the children were still expected to help with chores. Margaret in particular had a reputation as a disciplinarian, and had been described as not averse to using the rod on the Kelly children.

Education for a privileged Philadelphia girl like Grace Kelly started with the Sisters of the Assumption's all-girls Catholic school, Ravenhill Academy. She then went on to Stevens School, a private high school.

Grace Kelly as she is most famously remembered, is a slim blond with chiseled features, immaculate hair and chic clothes. Her look was carefully cultivated, celestial, and in the words of her frequent film collaborator, the legendary Alfred Hitchcock, she had "*sexual elegance.*" But in her younger years, this dreamy, immortal image of a stylish femme fatale was a lifetime away. She was a little bit on the heavy side, with glasses and a small bust. She had a thin, nasal voice. She was shy. But she eventually grew into the unabashed beauty she was always meant to be, and acting only buffered up her confidence. She had a real passion for it, and participated in productions within her East Falls, Philadelphia community on top of being in school plays. At The Little Theater in their upscale neighborhood, she participated in performances from the early age of 12 (some reports even say she started at 10). She also did some modeling and fashion events. Eventually, she never lacked for attention or admiration from young men.

Much harder to please were her parents. The Kelly household prized athletic achievement, and indeed, home movies of the four kids – a brother, Grace and her two sisters – would show them leaping from rooftops and racing. Her brother John Jr. would even go on to become an Olympic medalist himself. Grace, however, wasn't quite like her family and she did not have much of a heart for competitive sports. She was also sickly, and her nasal voice is said to have been the result of long bouts of head colds as a child. She was reportedly the least favored of the athletic, competitive Kelly siblings. It was in performing that she found her calling.

Jack and Margaret hoped she would outgrow her love of acting and perhaps settle down. By some accounts, Jack had looked down at the profession, allegedly seeing it as barely *"above streetwalker."* That fatherly approval never would come fully, even after all of Grace's successes. Some Hollywood pundits have even theorized that Grace Kelly's search for her father's approval led her to have romances with older men.

For Grace, the pull of performance and the arts remained strong in spite of her parent's lack of support. Ironically though, the arts were really in her blood and even in her name. She was named for her Aunt Grace, his father's sister, an actress who had died young. She had an uncle, Walter Kelly, who was an actor in vaudeville. Another uncle,

George Kelly, was a Pulitzer Prize-winning playwright.

After finishing high school, like many dreamers before her, Grace Kelly headed for the Big Apple. She enrolled at the American Academy of Dramatic Arts in 1947. Her parents were said to have wanted her to go to Bennington College, but her math skills were supposedly not up to par and she did not gain admission. Nevertheless, the Kellys did allow her New York move and schooling, but reportedly under the condition that she stayed at Manhattan's famous Barbizon Hotel.

Not just any hotel, the Barbizon was an institution, welcoming into its doors women with big dreams in the big city. It was like an incubator of female achievers, who could have some independence alongside a sense of safety (for some of the women, the rental bell still went to mommy and daddy even as they spread their wings pursuing careers as secretaries, models, actors, editors and other work in publishing – or finding a husband!). Some of the glitterati who 'graduated' from the single women's residence were Lauren Bacall, Joan Crawford, Candice Bergen, Cybill Shepherd, Joan Didion, Gene Tierney, Liza Minnelli and of course, Grace Kelly herself. Another of its famous residents, the iconic but ultimately tragic poet, Sylvia Plath, also called it home for a short time.

The Barbizon Hotel for Women stood at 23 stories high on the corner of East 63rd Street and Lexington Avenue in Manhattan. The 700-room hotel / dormitory was a fortress-like structure that opened in 1926 and indeed, approached the protection of the reputation of its young women with zeal. Applying for a spot could be tedious, and required multiple references, not to mention impeccable looks and demeanor. There were curfews and dress codes, and strict rules governing everything from food to the use of electrical appliances. Food was not allowed in the rooms and, just as prohibited were men. They were required to sign in upon entry and even then, were permitted only in a few public spaces; not that the spirited women of the Barbizon always followed this particular rule, for not a few of them have sneaked in the occasional guest.

It is delightful to imagine Grace Kelly in these gilded surroundings, cutting her teeth in New York in a prestigious address, amidst the energy of like-minded women. But even in a field of privilege, talent and ambition, someone always stands out from the rest and in many ways, Grace was among one of these. She was privileged, but she worked hard. And being a student at the American Academy of Dramatic Arts was tough. There was training for posture, manners, diction, pronunciation, control of movement, exercises for breathing, applying makeup, even walking and sitting down. The body was an instrument for communication.

While pursuing her craft, Grace Kelly also put her incredible looks to good use modeling, appearing in advertisements and on magazines. It supplemented her income, especially with limited financial support from her family. She was a pro, having been doing modeling since the age of 12.

Grace Kelly debuted on Broadway in 1949, for *The Father*. She was 19 years old. Her performance was found promising and fresh, and she was well-received not just by critics, but also by eagle-eyed television producers on the lookout for talent. The medium was on a post-war gold rush, and actresses for drama projects were in demand. Grace Kelly was beautiful, trained, professional, and had the grit for the demands of television. Over the early stages of her acting career, she would be credited in over 60 television dramas.

Though it was the stage that led her to the small screen, finding jobs on Broadway ultimately proved harder for her. It might have been her thin, nasal voice, which wasn't ideal for projecting in a theater. At least the stage led to small screen, and the small screen led her to the silver screen.

She acted in her first film, *Fourteen Hours* (1951) when she was 22. She had a minor role and was not particularly remarkable in it, especially by her own steep, artistic standards. She had a studio offer from her first Hollywood try, but the offer was not tempting enough for her to risk being typecast or limited. She decided to work on improving her acting instead, and returned to New York for further training and for the theater. She spent weeks in summer stock – theater productions in the professional off-season, held during the summer months – but Hollywood would soon come calling again.

Exactly how the newcomer got a plum part in *High Noon* (1952) is unclear, but by various reports, she was either approached by producer Stanley Kramer after seeing her in a production of *Elitch Gardens*; steered into the role by the famous actor Gary Cooper, who had seen something in her from her efforts in *Fourteen Hours*; or secured it after a meeting with director Fred Zinnemann; or perhaps all of the above. Either way, she secured the role of Amy Kane for *High Noon*. It wasn't just a minor role, either. She was going to play the veteran actor's wife and – spoiler alert! – buck against expectations and help save the day.

In the well-received Western, Grace Kelly played the tough town Marshal's young, new Quaker bride. She had a kind of posh, wooden, misplacedness that fit the role of a pacifist wife in the Wild West. The film would win Gary Cooper the Academy Award for Best Actor, but he was admirable in other ways. He was 28 years Kelly's senior, and he reportedly took the time to coach her. For Grace Kelly, though, it wasn't just a learning experience. Starring in *High Noon* brought her to the big leagues. It was just her second film, but she was already part of a movie that rapidly became a classic.

Soon, she was on a film set with established talent for Academy Award-winning director, John Ford's *Mogambo* (1953). As Linda Nordley, she is the fish-out-of-water in Kenya, vying for Clark Gable's big-game hunter against sultry socialite Ava Gardner. It was an important time in her career. She had landed a seven-year contract. For *Mogambo*, she would be nominated at the

Oscars for the first time, in the Supporting Actress category. She would also win a Best Supporting Actress nod from the Golden Globes. Grace Kelly was relatively new in Hollywood, but was quickly becoming known not only as a fine young beauty with elegance and poise, but also as an actress with a good grasp of her craft.

The acting accolades for *Mogambo* were reportedly a surprise for the actress, however. The self-critique is not new; in *High Noon*, she was reportedly dissatisfied with her performance and wanted to be better. She was always serious about performance, and never afraid of doing hard work. She would even insist on caveats within her MGM contract, to limit the number of pictures she made in a year so that she could also spend time in New York and hone her craft on stage. She was also protective of her image and the roles she played. Among her quirks were her general displeasure over publicity, her refusal to reveal her vital statistics (at the time, it was normal to do so), refusal to suffer an invasive makeover, and refusal to appear in B-movies. Even heavy makeup was a no-no. For example, in *To Catch a Thief*, she reportedly used no foundation, and could have makeup done in as little as seven minutes.

Over the course of her career, she stuck to her guns and showed willingness to suffer suspension to get her way. In days when the studios were the undisputed kings of Hollywood, the stars might have been packaged in wealth and glamour but they actually had very limited power in their creative lives. Many contracts bound talent

to projects designed around the studios'
goals for them. Refusal often meant not only
no pay, but also no permission to work
anywhere else. Suspension had very real
consequences for the present and future
income of an artist.

At the time it was practically unheard of in
Hollywood, for a young, relatively new
actress to not only have a desire to determine
her own creative fate, but also to have the
courage to assert herself and be willing to
lose opportunities, as well as risk her boss'
ire or her income. But Grace Kelly, by the
time she arrived in Tinsel Town, was already
her own woman. From her modeling work,
she knew how she wanted to look, and what
looked good on her. She was also financially
secure from her family wealth as well as her
own work outside of the movies, and she did

not need much money because she did not indulge in a lavish lifestyle in the first place. She was actually reportedly rather frugal – a trait she would always carry, as she was fond of reusing her wardrobe. She was also well-educated and well-raised. Thus, she had the privilege to say no to roles she did not like - an option she would exercise several times in her career. Her financial standing and courage allowed her to be selective with parts, and she would actually risk suspension for the role that would get her an Academy Award win for Best Actress in a Leading Role, for *The Country Girl* (1954).

As her star rose, Grace Kelly had a selection of offers, and would even turn down *On the Waterfront* (1954) with Marlon Brando. The role she had passed on, that of Edie Doyle, would secure the actress Eva Marie Saint an

Academy Award for Best Supporting Actress in 1955 – not that Grace Kelly had too much room for regret. That was the year she won the Oscar for her lead role in *The Country Girl*. She starred with established actors, Bing Crosby and William Holden, and played against type as an alcoholic has-been actor's drab wife. To secure the win, Kelly had to best trailblazing Dorothy Dandridge in *Carmen Jones*, iconic Judy Garland in *A Star Is Born*, and previous Oscar winners, Jane Wyman in *Magnificent Obsession*, and Audrey Hepburn in *Sabrina*.

She cemented her talent in *The Country Girl*, but Grace Kelly would best be remembered in her ice queen glory. And this image was best executed whenever she was in the creative path of suspense genius Alfred Hitchcock, for a string of critically-acclaimed and commercially-successful films, *Dial M for Murder* (1954), *Rear Window* (1954), and *To Catch a Thief* (1955).

Hollywood's Ice Queen

Alfred Hitchcock was once quoted as saying, *"It is ice that will burn your hands."*

The director had a well-deserved reputation as Hollywood's 'Master of Suspense.' He was known for his work in bold, thought-provoking movies with powerful, unforgettable imagery. He had a soft spot for a complex, icy blond hiding secrets and passions beneath her cool, aloof exterior – and Grace Kelly could have been born to work with him. Of the actress, he had once said that her frigidity was akin to *"…a mountain covered with snow, but that mountain was a volcano…"* In Alfred Hitchcock's hands, her icy sophistication was not brittle, but a powerful veneer. It wasn't shallow aloofness, it was deep restraint, and the filmmaker thrilled audiences with unfurling her complex layers.

In *Dial M for Murder*, she is Margot Wendice, adulterous wife to murderous husband, Tony Wendice (played by Oscar winner, Ray Milland). Tony is the frustrated mastermind trying to arrange his wealthy wife's death to get her money, but the hardier-than-expected Margot proves easier to frame for murder than to actually murder. In *Rear Window*, she plays socialite and all-around perfect girl, Lisa Carol Fremont opposite (another Oscar winning actor) James Stewart's wheelchair-bound ace photographer, L.B. Jeffries. L.B.'s temporary disability has him obsessed with watching his neighbors from his apartment window, and is soon convinced there is foul play going on between a husband and wife across the street. Lisa does the legwork as his surprisingly courageous and adventurous partner in solving the crime. In *To Catch a Thief*, Grace Kelly's final film with Hitchcock, she stars opposite Cary Grant's reformed cat burglar, John Robie, as the privileged Frances Stevens. Frances and her mother, a wealthy widow, become the target of a Robie copycat while vacationing in the French Riviera. Sparks fly between Robie and the perceptive, seductive Frances – until the Stevens' jewels are lost and suspicions fall on Robie.

Grace Kelly was luminous and unforgettable in all these films, Hitchcock adored having her in them, and the work arrangements also worked out for her studio, MGM. They were making money loaning her talents out to the filmmaker. Indeed, the collaboration seemed favorable to all parties. For Grace, working with Hitchcock allowed her some leeway against simply giving in to her contractual obligations of accepting any and all studio-assigned parts. As for what Hitchcock saw…

Around the time he was casting for *Dial M…*, Hitchcock screened *Mogambo* but was reportedly unimpressed by Grace Kelly, especially by her voice. But he did look at Kelly's *Taxi* screen test (a part she lost to actress Constance Smith), and was intrigued enough to want to meet with her. He saw for himself her dreamy blond beauty but also her restraint and underlying sexual allure. He saw a kind of duality in her that would be cultivated in *Dial M…*, as she played prim wife one moment, sensual adulteress in the next.

Alfred Hitchcock could be overwhelming for his leading ladies (some say, even abusive), but he and Grace worked well together. He had patience with the actress, and she was willing to learn from him. They also shared a sense of humor. Creatively, Hitchcock and Kelly both carried a theater approach into their film work. *Dial M...*, after all, had been a play acquired by Hitchcock for film, and he very much intended to bring in that same constrained quality into his movie. It was in a sense, a filmed play – which likely resonated with an actress like Grace Kelly, who held theater in high regard. Her dramatic training came in handy too, as *Dial M...* had her acting with her whole body, with some scenes not even showing her face.

Hitchcock found himself a muse, and reportedly had Grace early in his sights for his next project, even before production for *Dial M...* was finished. This next project was *Rear Window*, and Grace would reportedly pass on *On the Waterfront* with Marlon Brando to work with Hitchcock again.

Rear Window is based on a short story by Cornell Woolrich, which then initially came into the hands of Joshua Logan, before being firmly held by radio writer John Michael Hayes as scriptwriter. Grace Kelly's Lisa was an addition to the original, and the character was basically designed around her. Hitchcock had even arranged for Hayes to spend time with Kelly and include some of her traits in the writing. The result was a character who had some of Grace Kelly's true self in it, and some of Hayes' wife, who was also a former model. And so in Lisa Carol Fremont, it's as if we see Grace Kelly herself unfurl; a lively girl of warmth and humor beneath an icy, sophisticated, oh-so-perfect (perhaps too perfect) façade.

Next on the pipeline for the formidable pair was *To Catch a Thief*, based on a novel by David Dodge. Again, Hitchcock had Grace Kelly in mind early on – a choice shared by the movie's principal actor, Cary Grant, who was open in his admiration of her skill and control as an actress. MGM loaned her to Hitchcock and Paramount for the project (getting something in exchange of course, in this case, the talents of hot actor William Holden). The film is lighter than the usual Hitchcock fare, a charming, breezy production filmed for the most part, on location in the South of France. Grace Kelly was, as usual, exquisite in her ice cold glory and subtly unfolding, well-paced, surprising sexiness. She was classy but sensual, bright and funny – some would say, simply perfect. The ideal woman.

Well-received though it was, *To Catch a Thief* was the last of their projects together, and Hitchcock would seek his ideal, icy femme fatale elsewhere afterwards. The director liked having complex blondes in his films for a miscellany of declared and theorized reasons, among them that (1) they photographed well in black and white; (2) that gradual breaking of their cool veneer as a character becomes more articulated, tended to up the surprise factor in a movie; and (3) they represented perfect women he could completely control where he otherwise would not have been able to attain them. The last is a theory that is inspired by his overbearing, controlling, almost obsessive approach upon the actresses on his films. With Grace Kelly though, he was said to have been mostly a gentleman, and had even been willing to listen to her input. This was a rarity, especially as it required the director to make adjustments from his meticulously-set scenes to adhere to her suggestions.

After Hitchcock's three-picture collaboration with Grace Kelly, he tried to capture that same magic with the archetype that would eventually be known as The Hitchcock Blonde – characters that are complex, mysterious, perhaps a little duplicitous, who were played by an icy, stunning blond actress. Among them were Kim Novak in *Vertigo* (1958); Eva Marie Saint in *North by Northwest* (1959); Janet Leigh in *Psycho* (1960); and Tippi Hedren in *The Birds* (1963) and *Marnie* (1964).

How Grace Kelly could have embodied iconic roles like these in such unforgettable movies, we will never know… for she would leave Hollywood all too soon to play the biggest part of her life. That of Princess Grace of Monaco.

A Reel and Real Femme Fatale

Younger generations would know Grace Kelly best for her glamorous, royal persona. She was that unflappable blond who captured audiences in Hollywood and turned away from Tinsel Town to win the heart of a real prince. She even looked as if she was born to be a princess.

The sad truth is that many beautiful women come and go in Hollywood, and even those who have accolades and talent to match their beauty do not always have enduring relevance or continuing cultural impact. In short - beauty and talent just aren't enough to create a legend. In the case of Grace Kelly though, her status as Hollywood legend is, ironically because first, she was willing to leave it behind. It wasn't just about leaving it *at her prime* to become a princess, note – she had always showed courage in risking opportunities and income in pursuit of a worthy and challenging part. Second, in a land of naked opportunists and publicity-hungry performers, she always showed a preference for keeping many aspects of her life private. Like the roles that would define her, she had control and restraint… and she also had complexity and secrets.

Grace Kelly won audiences with her icy beauty and red hot talent. She'd won over her directors and her co-stars too, who praised her humor, hard work, professionalism and thoroughness. But in her private life, she would also win over a collection of lovers. She had so many real and rumored conquests, that tales of wild, romantic exploits would spread about her, including allegations of nymphomania. In her beautiful, swanlike wake, she may have left behind broken hearts and broken marriages.

The rogue's gallery of Kelly's alleged lovers gives passing mention to her early conquests when she was a young woman finding her way in New York. Here, it is said that she dated fellow young actors and classmates. But one of the most controversial figures in her dating history was acting instructor, Don Richardson.

He was only 28 when they were in each other's lives, but Don Richardson would go on to have a long and respectable career in the arts. When he passed away in 1996, he left behind 50 years of work as an acting teacher and as a director on Broadway and television. He also wrote a book, *Acting Without Agony: An Alternative to the Method*, that is used all over the world. Over his years as an instructor, he counted among his students the likes of Anne Bancroft, Elizabeth Montgomery, Zero Mostel and, famously Grace Kelly. She was only 17 years old when she came into the American Academy of Dramatic Arts in New York.

Some have credited Richardson for the making of Grace Kelly as she is known; though this feat, of course, could also be said of her Pulitzer Prize-winning Uncle George

Kelly who nurtured her love of the arts and whose name supposedly got her foot in the door. It could also be said of director Alfred Hitchcock, who taught her about filmmaking and captured her most iconic images. It could even be said of designer and eventual boyfriend Oleg Cassini, who had helped style her. Grace Kelly is clearly an agglomeration of what is desirable to many men, who may have each had a contribution in the graceful final product. For his part, Richardson is reputed to have influenced Grace Kelly in important ways in her student years in New York. They dated for a few years after all, with a large gap in their age and experience. He was also, at the end of the day, an educator. It makes sense that he would have had some expertise to share.

Richardson is said to have helped her by securing her first agent, and by helping her get her first Broadway role in *The Father*. He may have also been the one to steer her away from her Philadelphia accent. It is unverified how far his influence went or how much of a Pygmalion he was to the early incarnation of Grace Kelly, but what is certain is that Richardson recognized her ambition, and always thought she showed promise of stardom.

Their affair, however, had a much bleaker future than her acting career. When she brought him to Philadelphia to meet her family, he was practically turned out. Her father, the already-impossible to please John Kelly, allegedly had an anti-Semitic streak to boot, which did not bode well for Richardson even before the family's distressful discovery of his still-upcoming divorce. If rumors hold true, Richardson would eventually even be offered a luxury vehicle by the older Kellys - a Jaguar! - if he would just leave Grace alone. It was declined, but the relationship would nevertheless still end.

Some say Grace Kelly had only used Richardson only as a stepping stone to feed her hungry ambition. Then again, some people also said she liked dancing nude to Hawaiian music, and other stories would have her dancing in her underwear at the halls of the legendary Barbizon Hotel. Another tale has her modeling lingerie in New York, and popping by a lover's apartment during break time. And did she really romance the Waldorf Astoria's maître d'? The goal, allegedly being that of finding opportunities to connect with influential men who could boost her career. If the hotel maître d' wasn't spared her charms, it should come as no surprise that she was also allegedly able to romance married men. If you looked at source after source speculating on Grace Kelly's alleged love affairs, they read just like her resume. Could she really have romanced so many of the men she co-starred with?

She starred in *High Noon* with actor Gary Cooper and director Fred Zinnermann; rumors are that she ended up romancing them both. Cooper, at the time, was reportedly married but separated and in a relationship with another actress, Patricia Neal. But he did fit into the mold that was allegedly Grace Kelly's romantic weakness;

he was much older (28 years her senior) and somewhat of a fatherly figure.

Next she was in *Mogambo* with Clark Gable (who is also 28 years older than she). Grace Kelly has been quoted as saying something to the effect of, 'what else was there to do in a tent in Africa with Clark Gable?' But is the quote accurate and even if it were, was she being serious considering she had a wicked, mischievous sense of humor? And if the answer to these questions are yes, how far into the off-screen did they really take their onscreen romance?

In *Dial M for Murder*, director Alfred Hitchcock reportedly had an unhealthy infatuation for her, but it is not known if and how she may have encouraged it, or if she reciprocated in any way. But that is only just one of the rumors about Kelly's romantic and / or sexual entanglements in this film. Her co-star, Oscar winner, Ray Milland (24 years her senior), is said to have fallen deeply in love with her and she, with him. The snag? He's long been married to Muriel Weber, and they had children together. But did his wife Muriel really kick him out? And did Kelly and Milland live together in a shared apartment and considered getting married, as has been suggested by gossip? Did Kelly deserve the antagonistic wave in the Hollywood community that followed these rumors, and to be called a homewrecker for it? Did her actions really merit gossip columnist and entertainment icon, Hedda Hopper's label of a nymphomaniac?

Grace was reportedly shocked and unprepared for the vitriol against her following the Milland situation. Hollywood pundits would later note that she had 'a healthy sexual appetite,' and was not a promiscuous type; she really seemed to be looking for affection, approval and love. The antagonism probably stemmed from the wide disparity between the image she projected, as best symbolized by her fancy white gloves, with her scandalous private life.

Unfortunately after all that grief, Milland still wasn't The One. Either by Kelly family interference, or Milland's lingering affection for his wife, or Milland's realization of the ghastly financial impact a divorce would have on him (with properties apparently made out in Muriel's name!), or a combination of all three, the romance fizzled out. Milland went back to his wife and would be with her until his death in 1986, while Grace Kelly sashayed her way into another controversial romantic dalliance.

Hollywood playboy, William Holden (11 years older than the actress), would also have a shot with the ice queen, for he starred with Grace Kelly in both *The Bridges at Toko-Ri* (1954) and *The Country Girl*. At the time, Holden was married to his long-suffering wife, actress Brenda "Ardis" Marshall, who was reportedly aware of her husband's indiscretions. Holden and Kelly allegedly had a steamy affair, cut short only because he had previously had a vasectomy. Interestingly enough, a similar rumor follows William Holden and actress Audrey Hepburn, with whom he starred in *Sabrina*

(1954); co-stars madly in love, Holden willing to leave his wife, a break-up after his vasectomy is discovered... which shows that perhaps, rumors are really rather difficult to believe. Perhaps Grace Kelly was, as some sources note, just on the rebound from Ray Milland.

Another theory is that Holden and Kelly's romance ended because of Bing Crosby. The three were co-stars in *The Country Girl*, and Crosby and Kelly got along swimmingly even if Crosby did not originally want Grace Kelly for the role of his wife. He thought she was too beautiful and was skeptical her acting abilities could handle the heavyweight part (of course, she would end up winning an Academy Award for it). Holden, if rumors are true, may have stepped down for Crosby, who was a massive crossover superstar. Crosby, a recent widower, was in high demand in film, music, and radio. He was an Oscar winner and a chart-topper, with more hits than The Beatles or Elvis. Holden may have backed away to avoid a collision he likely would have lost if Crosby decided to push his considerable weight.

Not that the Crosby-Kelly romance had much steam. Their romance would end, allegedly due to Marlon Brando; though rumors of Crosby catching them in bed after the Academy Awards (in which Kelly won for *The Country Girl* and Brando took home the Best Actor trophy for *On the Waterfront*), just seems too unlikely. Kelly and Crosby worked together again in her last film before she left Hollywood behind though – *High Society* (1956). They settled with being close friends, and he would even help her land a hit song, via their duet, the soundtrack *True Love*. Another cast member, however, would allegedly capture Grace's attention – she may have explored a relationship with Frank Sinatra, too.

Non-actors would make it to Grace Kelly's hit list, via the successful designer, Oleg Cassini. Cassini had been hit hard by Kelly-fever after *Mogambo*, and he was determined to have her. He reportedly even sent her roses every day until she agreed to a meal with him. He was doing well in his field (and would famously dress First Lady of the United States and style icon, Jackie Kennedy), and came from a line of Russian aristocrats. He had a hand in her styling, adding some sexuality to her look. Grace was reportedly interested in marrying him (he later said they were in love and engaged). His romantic history, however, was less than impressive to the Kelly matriarch, what with divorces and children. Though he was technically free to have a relationship with Grace Kelly, innuendo wouldn't escape this pair either, and rumors of pregnancy and abortion would be linked to them.

Royalty also wouldn't escape a Grace Kelly connection, even before Prince Rainier III of Monaco swept her away to his principality. The Shah of Iran might have been a suitor, as well as Prince Aly Kahn. American political royalty may have also been in the actress' sphere, as she was rumored to have dated John F. Kennedy.

Other men would be connected to Grace Kelly aside from these; photos of the actress with French actor Jean-Pierre Aumont would come out in the tabloids too, and actor David Niven once recalled almost saying "Grace Kelly" when asked by Prince Rainier about exciting lovers. A few other names would pop up in rumor and innuendo – Richard Boccelli, Tony Curtis, Cary Grant, Anthony Havelock-Allan, Gene Lyons, James Stewart, Sidney Wood… and these are only the prominent men. There were allegedly unknown others.

So with this rather lengthy list of alleged conquests, was Grace Kelly a misunderstood flirt or some sort of a sex addict? Was she really looking for the love of a father figure in every man? Who in her list of alleged conquests are true and who are false and to what extent? Was she looking for sex or romance? Was she naïve or promiscuous? She definitely had mystique, and the racy stories about her sometimes border on the fantastic and unbelievable. Could these crazy rumors even be just a little bit true? Or has she perhaps captured everyone in a collective fantasy of imagining the prim, glacial blond in the most unlikely of sexual scenarios?

Was there really a simmering siren underneath all that ice?

She had ensnared legendary Alfred Hitchcock in that irresistible duality, and he in turn had helped perpetuate that fantasy via unforgettable movie magic. It seems then, that the public can never truly know 'the real' Grace Kelly under all that ice.

Letters written by Grace Kelly to her personal secretary and good friend, Prudence Wise, would be made available at auction a few years after her death. The correspondence spanned two decades, covering some of Grace Kelly's most exciting periods in Hollywood. They were pretty candid, and discussed her co-stars and alleged lovers in warm, friendly terms. When asked, a representative from the owner of the collection said that there seemed to be no hints of romance with anyone other than Clark Gable. Could it be then, that all of these affairs are really unsubstantiated, or did she just not confide about them?

The actress was never afraid of keeping some things to herself and there are many secrets she would take to the grave. In addressing some of the rumors about her, she'd simply said in general terms, that as an unmarried women, she was perceived as a threat. Whether or not that threat was actualized and with whom, we might never know. That sense of mystery, that tease, is part of her enduring appeal.

Princess Grace of Monaco

In the mid-1950s, Grace Kelly was at a turning point in her life.

She didn't know it yet, but she had already made most of the movies that would make up her filmography: her 1951 debut, *Fourteen Hours*; her instant Western classic, *High Noon* in 1952; her critically acclaimed acting performance for *Mogambo* in 1953; her Oscar winning turn in *The Country Girl* (1954); her iconic icy moments as Alfred Hitchcock's muse in *Dial M for Murder* (1954), *Rear Window* (1954), and *To Catch a Thief* (1955); and the average *Green Fire* (1954) and *The Bridges at Toko-Ri* (1954). She found that her Academy Award win didn't quite lead to parts that compelled her, and she was also dissatisfied with her personal life while her sisters were well-settled with families of their own.

It was at these professional and personal crossroads that she would meet Prince Charming.

A Royal Romance

The romance between Grace Kelly and her Prince had a glamorous start. The setting? It was 1955, and Grace was in France for the Cannes Film Festival as part of the American delegation. Oscar winning actress Olivia de Havilland and her new husband, *Paris-Match* editor Pierre Galante, convinced Grace to visit Monaco for an audience and photo session with Prince Rainer III.

Fate was feeling a little mischievous that day, and Grace was beset by small inconveniences on her way to her date with destiny. Her hotel suffered in an electricity strike, which prevented her from preparing properly. Instead of a hair dryer, she had to settle for a floral headband. Instead of a pressed attire, she had to settle for a dress she was not confident in. There was a fender-bender. The Prince himself arrived late, nearly missing the Hollywood superstar.

But meet they did, and the rest is history…

… or, not quite. For complex and compelling public figures, love and marriage can never be quite so straightforward. Prince Rainier, born on the 31st of May, 1923, had been sitting on the throne since the age of 26. He was 32 when he met Grace Kelly and eager for a bride. Over the years, he was said to be aware of the increasing need to start a family and produce an heir, which was necessary for Monaco to continue to be independent. For a long time, he had been in a relationship with actress Gisele Pascal, but he had big ambitions that did not quite have a place for her. They broke up and she married and started a family with another actor. Rainier, on the other hand, started nurturing his big dreams for Monaco and navigating how to get there with the perfect Princess.

The Catholic Rainier had an unexpected matchmaker on his side. His spiritual advisor, Father Tucker, looked into the possibilities of the Prince's union with other Catholic girls, including Grace Kelly. She was beautiful, accomplished, classy, and like Rainier, raised devout. It certainly helped that their first meeting left them both intrigued by the other, and they managed to keep a lively correspondence even when she left and returned to the United States. It was also somewhat fortuitous that Grace Kelly's next movie was *The Swan* (1956) – where she played a Princess.

Later that year, Prince Rainier visited the United States for a diplomatic tour… and a proposal! Monaco wasn't very well-known in the country at the time, but the impossible-to-impress Jack and Margaret Kelly suddenly had a titled aristocrat from an old European family asking for their daughter's hand in marriage, and probably for the first time, they were ready to approve of their middle daughter's life choices. Even her Oscar for *The Country Girl* had proved not particularly moving for them, but Prince

Rainier III and what he could do for the family's standing in Philadelphia was definitely something the Kelly couple could be proud of. But before anything else, Grace Kelly reportedly had to be checked for fertility, and the matter of her infamous $2 million dowry (to cover part of the wedding costs had to be resolved. Good thing Jack Kelly was a multi-millionaire and wanted his daughter to be a princess.

There was also the issue of her career – Rainier found it improper for his royal bride to continue to be in the movies and as a matter of fact, Grace Kelly's films would eventually be banned in Monaco. But Grace moved forward with the union, reportedly in the hopes that she might one day be able to change his mind.

Soon enough, all signs were pointing go, even if the couple had not known each other for very long. Maybe she married the Prince to please her father. Maybe she went through with it because she didn't know she could never return to acting. As for Rainier, maybe he was in a rush to marry the paper and picture perfect bride to be his Princess and make an heir. Maybe he saw the perfect complement for his dreams for his country. Then again, maybe they really were madly in love.

Either way – being Princess of Monaco brought Grace Kelly into her Third Act. She'd already leapt from stage and television to the giant, intimidating sea of Hollywood. Now she was on the curious intersection between politics and entertainment. She was entering the world of old world royalty.

A public announcement of the engagement was made in the Kelly's stately Philadelphia home. And that staple of royal romances everywhere, a breathtaking engagement ring, was featured on the beautiful bride-to-be's famously elegant and expressive hand. The ring is a huge 10.47-carat, emerald-cut diamond on a platinum band. It stars alongside Kelly in her las feature film, *High Society*, where it catches the audience's attention as Bing Crosby's character famously remarks, "*Some stone, did you mine it yourself?*"

Grace Kelly capped off her Hollywood career by playing socialite Tracy Lord in *High Society*, and then she was off to Monaco with her family for the so-called 'wedding of the century.' Her mother Margaret Kelly was reportedly disappointed that the ceremony, held on the 19th of April, 1956, wouldn't be before the family's peers (and snobbish critics!) in Philadelphia. It may have comforted her to know that few in America could have missed it. MGM, which proved amenable to their star's early Hollywood exit especially since they were getting exclusive rights to film her wedding, would make footage accessible to a wide audience. There were 600 guests at the event, but a whole lot more people lined the streets to cheer the couple (20,000 by some estimates), and even more were able to catch it on television; *The Wedding in Monaco* captured a 30 million-strong TV audience when it aired. The studio was also generous to their star, and sent her off with a bonus, her character Tracy Lord's *High Society* wardrobe, and the unforgettable

Helen Rose creation that would make wedding history.

Long after the wedding, the gown designed by MGM's wardrobe wizard spent some time in the Philadelphia Museum of Art, and it was a much deserved place. It really is a piece of art, this $8,000 silk taffeta dress with antique rose-point lace and pearls, which took three dozen seamstresses, six weeks to make. It was well worth the effort and attention; ever since Grace walked down the aisle in it, it has become *the* wedding gown to judge all royal wedding gowns to come after it, including the recent breathtaking, Sarah Burton for Alexander McQueen piece worn by Catherine Middleton, when she married Prince William in England in 2011.

Royal on the Rise

By her marriage to Rainier, Grace had acquired a multitude of titles aside from "Princess of Monaco." She was Princess Chateau-Porciean too, and several times over each: a duchess, a countess, a marquise, and a baroness. She had joined an esteemed line of aristocrats. Her husband's family, the Grimaldis, is among the oldest ruling European families, and have been connected to Monaco since 1297.

Her new home is the world's second smallest country, undersized only by the Vatican. It is so small that the land area is about the size of Central Park in Manhattan. One of the biggest attractions here is the Casino Monte Carlo, which actually bars Monegasque citizens, for gambling is illegal to them.

Gambling revenues from visiting foreigners is limited, accounting for a small percentage of the economy. A larger chunk comes from tourism and why shouldn't it? Tourists may want to see the principality for themselves, what with cinematic icons like Iron Man (in *Iron Man 3*) and James Bond visiting often (in *Never Say Never* Again, *Golden Eye* and *Casino Royale*) onscreen. Monaco does not collect income taxes and has a reputation for being a tax haven. Its citizens enjoy a high standard of living, and many millionaires and billionaires either call it home, or use it as a playground – among them, Bono and George Clooney. Some of its most glamorous events are the Monaco Grand Prix, and the Monaco Yacht Show.

It wasn't always this way. Though the tiny country was beautiful and the Grimaldi family ruling it was well-established, the postwar economics were not very sound. When Prince Rainier came to the throne in 1949, the aging casinos, hotels and tourist attractions were experiencing staggering losses. Competition with other locales for gambling and tourism was fierce. In the first years of the 1950s, the Societe Monegasque de Banques et de Metaux Precieux, went bankrupt. Monaco seemed to need an invigorating shot in the arm.

According to legend, Greek magnate Aristotle Onassis conceived of the idea that Monaco's Prince Rainier III should marry a superstar, and put the country back on the map. If that's not even more fantastic, the suggested star had been no one less than Marilyn Monroe (who was reportedly not inclined to cooperate). Whether or not this is true or if the Prince Rainier had even known about it, is uncertain. Either way, whether or not by design, the desired effect was accomplished by Rainier's marriage to Grace Kelly, which did have an important impact on the country.

The 'wedding of the century' certainly increased tourism revenues. But she also gave Monaco recall and prestige, and indirectly, helped increase flows of capital into the country which in turn, stimulated it to modernize, attract other investments, and decrease its reliance on gambling income. With Grace's ambassadorial image and Rainier's daring vision, Monaco's economy became more diverse and it flourished for a long time. The government coffers had funds, even social security made money, and unemployment was stunningly low.

It is hard to imagine a setting and lifestyle more fitting to someone of Grace Kelly's wealth, style and elegance. It certainly seemed like an ideal home for a 26-year-old American Princess. But at the beginning, it wasn't the case at all. Grace reportedly did not connect very well with the Grimaldis, save perhaps for her husband's father, Prince Pierre. Rainier's mother, Princess Charlotte, as well as his sister, Princess Antoinette, were said to be more lukewarm in their reception of the actress. Grace also found life in her new home difficult. Before becoming its ruler's wife, she had only visited once after all. She knew some of French but the language and accent in Monaco proved challenging to her. She also suffered from depression after giving birth, and after having miscarriages. Her father Jack's death in 1960 also compounded her tumultuous feelings at the early period of her marriage.

Prince Rainier tried his best to help his wife, and though he had banned her films in his country after they were married, he was reportedly initially supportive of her return to the screen. She was, after all, an artist. She was proud of her work, and it couldn't have been easy turning away from the passion for performance that she's had and fought for since she was a child. That she had to leave acting behind was probably one of her few regrets.

The question was, however, what would be a comeback worthy of her Serene Highness, the Princess of Monaco? Even after years away from the movies, Grace Kelly could still have had her pick of parts. But there was one man who had an edge above the competition – visionary filmmaker, the Master of Suspense himself, Alfred Hitchcock.

Hitchcock adored his seminal icy blond, and even pursued her after her royal retirement – discreetly, of course, out of deference to her new status as a princess. He had purchased rights to bring to life the Winston Graham novel *Marnie* (1964) on film, but could not find the right actress. He eventually imagined it to be Grace Kelly's comeback film, and went through her agents for them to pass it on to her. Hitchcock claimed never to have broached the topic directly to Kelly, even if he did see her and her husband several times while in France. The princess not only agreed to do it, it had even been announced by a Monaco palace official in 1962.

Unfortunately, she would eventually withdraw. The official reason was scheduling conflict… but there could have been many other possible obstructions to her return to the big screens. First, there was some confusion on her contractual obligations with MGM – was her relationship with them terminated or merely suspended when she retired from acting in 1956? Were they, therefore, entitled to demand participation in Hitchcock's project? Second, there was also a question of the Princess' salary – how much would it be, and / or would there be a share of the profits? The question of money ushered in an entirely new issue all on its own – was Monaco in financial straits, such that the

Princess needed to return to filmmaking to help them along? This last one had to be addressed decisively, and Rainier and Grace would say that the film project coincided with Grace's plans to spend time with her family in America. Furthermore, they claimed the funds would be used for charity.

Not to be left out of consideration were the opinions of the press and the people. There wasn't just speculation on why Princess Grace was returning to work, there was also criticism of it. Apparently, the citizens of Monaco had qualms about their princess playing a woman of questionable morals on screen. There may have also been pressure from her husband and / or France's Charles de Gaulle and / or conservative and powerful voices in Monaco, against her return to film in this incarnation, or in any incarnation. The timing may have actually been bad too, either way – Hitchcock postponed work on *Marnie* due to the small gap between its start and the completion of Hitchcock's work on *The Birds*, which could have steered the schedule away from Grace's family visit to America. Politics may have also played a part – around that time, France was exerting pressure on Monaco regarding its tax system, and was holding over its head the conclusion of a treaty that would have affected such pivotal things as water and electric supply if it was not re-negotiated. Rainier, therefore, could not leave until the matter was settled and neither could his wife.

For whatever reason then, whether or not it was from a single cause or a confluence of events, Princess Grace bowed out of *Marnie* and the role eventually went to Tippi Hedren, another icy blond who had worked with Alfred Hitchcock previously on *The Birds* (1963).

The *Marnie* fallout pretty much cemented how far removed Grace Kelly had become, from the possibility of ever returning to her old life as an actress. She reportedly pondered and privately lamented the roles she could have played and the great movies she could have made, but she made do and moved on. She devoted her time in Monaco to her role as Princess, and it was very much a role indeed, for she would employ the same techniques that she did in her craft in its execution. She researched the part, modified her behavior, and became very much the conservative royal.

Perhaps her legendary film collaborator, Alfred Hitchcock really did understand her well because when he was first asked to react to news of her engagement, he expressed happiness that Grace Kelly had secured *"such a good part."*

She approached royalty like acting work, and Grace Kelly always was very hard working and professional. According to reports, a typical day for the Princess would start as early as 7:15 AM, spent on her desk for several hours before she received guests and visitors at the palace. The rest of the day was spent making or listening to presentations, and appearances at benefits and galas for a miscellany of charities and projects. Her charitable endeavors included heading the Monaco Red Cross, founding AMADE Mondiale (a charitable organization focusing on the needs and rights of children all over the world), and advocating for special needs in Monaco. She also found a way to infuse her love of the arts with her role as a Princess; she helped protect and preserve historic structures, and became a patron of the arts. Her projects included festivals and fundraisers that are still running up to now.

She accomplished many things, even while she coped with difficulties in her home life. She and her Prince Charming would actually eventually spend much of their latter years apart. There were rumors of marital tension and affairs, though many in their inner circle would say they had a relatively solid partnership.

The children were also somewhat problematic. Their eldest, Princess Caroline, married a French playboy in 1978 and divorced him in 1980. Her romantic troubles would keep her father's hands full even after Grace passed away with a marriage that ended in a tragic accident, and her current, troubled one with Prince Ernst August of Hanover. Stephanie also proved difficult after Grace's tragic death, with controversial and short-lived romances featuring her bodyguard, an elephant trainer, and an acrobat. Prince Albert, who would succeed his father in 2005, also has his own woes, which includes illegitimate children and rumors of his bride trying to run away. As of this writing though, they are still together and have young twins.

Legacy

Can you really be a Hollywood legend, when your film career is basically comprised of a few good years and barely a dozen films? Where many of them are in the supporting role? Where the role that got you an Academy Award is actually how you are least remembered? Where you retired from the movies at age 26? It was a film career cut short no matter which way you look at it – as high as its trajectory it might have been, as magically as it might have ended.

It wasn't just her Hollywood career that would come to an abrupt halt. Grace Kelly, at the age of just 52, passed away in 1982 when she suffered a stroke while driving a car in Monaco. Her daughter Stephanie was with her when their car swerved off a treacherous coastal road and slid down the mountainside. Stephanie was hurt but not too seriously. Grace, on the other hand, would never regain consciousness and died soon afterwards. Her very life was cut tragically short.

And yet with these short years she still remains one of the most interesting public figures to have ever walked the Earth. Tributes to Grace Kelly can be found across continents. There is of course, the coveted Hermes Kelly bag, once known as the Haut a Courroie, renamed for the woman who was popularly seen and photographed with the iconic purse, especially as she used it to hide her baby bump from the press. In the United States, she was the first actress on a postage stamp, issued in 1993. In 2007, two-euro commemorative coins featured her profile. And in a move that might finally have pleased her father, Jack B. Kelly, the Henley Royal Regatta, an esteemed rowing event, renamed a women's race after her – The Princess Grace Challenge Cup. She is widely considered to be one of the greatest female stars of all time, including by the American Film Institute. Her memorabilia continues to attract vast sums at auctions, and every once in a while, a fresh new facet of her personality comes out, capturing our attention again. In that gradual, carefully controlled and restrained Grace Kelly way – she unfurls again, showing us more of herself through recovered letters, collectibles and accounts of friends.

It has been revealed that she remained very down to earth, and had a pragmatic mind.

She valued her family and her past, and would even return constantly to Philadelphia visiting the St. Bridget Catholic Church where she was baptized and where her family worshipped. She had a famous sense of humor and was known to indulge in a bawdy joke or a hearty laugh. Just as in her Hollywood career, she was not comfortable wearing heavy makeup in her daily life. One of the world's most stylish women not only when she was alive but up to the present, was actually not often in designer clothes. She was comfortable wearing simple pieces by the local seamstresses of Monaco, and famously reused clothes, sometimes for years on end. They could be anything from a beloved coat, to her maternity wear and yes, even the dress she won her Academy Award in. She loved games like charades, and had a passion for astrology. She kept her hands busy with handicrafts like knitting, crochet and pottery, and she loved tooling around in the soil, for she had a passion for gardening. The world often saw her and currently remembers her for her white gloves, but her hands have also been happily shoved into gardening gloves digging into soil. She kept her artist's heart, and found shared interests with talented eccentrics like the surrealist artist, Salvador Dali. And why not? She could have a connection with people in spite of her glacial, perfect countenance. She even knew how to manage the notoriously difficult Alfred Hitchcock. She was also not averse to spending time with common folk, and continued to make time for fans. According to a close confidant of the Princess, one particularly devoted supporter would be in the royal's audience once a year, swapping stories over tea.

These were the little things behind the imposing image of the ice queen. At the end of the day, she was a hometown girl who did good in Philadelphia, and who did her best to please her parents. She tried to maximize her talents wherever she found herself – on the stage, on the small screen, on the silver screen, in the role of a Princess, wife, and mother. She was open with love and affection, and she was fearless in the pursuit of what she wanted and felt she deserved. She had accomplished so much in the short time she inhabited all her incarnations.

Perhaps it is a reminder that life is not about length, but about the meaning you put into it. That it's not about the years, but about the passions you pursue, the love you seek and give, the light you shed, the art you share, the inspiration you ignite. Because if life were measured by these things, Grace Kelly continues to live on, and will outlive many of us.

Made in the USA
Las Vegas, NV
20 March 2022

45997176R10059